THE SECRET TO SELF-LOVE AND GROWTH

COPYRIGHT © 2023 Edward M. Farney

TABLE OF CONTENT

The Power of Acceptance

The idea of accepting oneself may seem like a straightforward concept, but in reality, it can be a challenging process to implement. Accepting and embracing oneself completely, including both strengths and weaknesses, is a fundamental aspect of developing self-love and personal growth. This chapter explores the importance of self-acceptance and provides practical strategies for integrating it into your daily life.

Self-acceptance is not just a nice-to-have quality; it has a significant impact on your overall well-being and quality of life. Studies have shown that self-acceptance is linked to greater resilience, improved relationships, and reduced levels of stress and anxiety. By accepting yourself, you are more likely to make decisions that align with your values and goals, rather than conform to external expectations. Additionally, self-acceptance can increase your compassion and kindness towards yourself, leading to a boost in confidence and self-esteem.

Despite the numerous advantages of self-acceptance, it can be challenging to put into practice. Many of us have internalized negative messages from our peers, family, or society that make us feel inadequate. An inner critical voice can continually remind us that we are not smart, attractive, or talented enough. It can be difficult to break free from these negative patterns of thinking and learn to embrace ourselves for who we are.

Fortunately, self-acceptance is a skill that can be cultivated over time. Here are some practical strategies for developing self-acceptance:

Firstly, mindfulness is the practice of being present at the moment, observing your thoughts and emotions without judgment. Mindfulness allows you to become more aware of negative self-talk and learn to let it go, rather than getting caught up in it. Mindfulness also enables you to appreciate the present moment and the beauty in yourself and your surroundings.

Secondly, identifying your strengths is crucial. We all have unique talents and strengths, but it can be easy to overlook them when we are focused on our flaws. Take some time to reflect on your strengths, whether it is your sense of humor, creativity, or listening skills. Focusing on your strengths will enable you to see yourself in a more positive light.

Thirdly, challenge negative self-talk by questioning its validity. When you notice negative self-talk, challenge it with evidence to the contrary. For example, if you think "I'm not good enough," remind yourself of times when you have succeeded in the past. Consider what evidence you have to support the negative thought and whether there is any evidence to suggest the opposite is true.

Fourthly, practicing self-compassion involves treating yourself with the same kindness and empathy you would extend to a friend. When you make a mistake or experience a setback, respond to yourself with kindness rather than harsh self-criticism. Recognize that everyone makes mistakes, and failure is an opportunity for growth and learning.

Fifthly, embrace imperfection as part of what makes you unique and interesting. It's natural to want to be perfect, but no one is perfect. Learn to see mistakes and failures as opportunities to learn and grow, rather than as signs of weakness.

Lastly, seek support from friends, family members, or a therapist as you work on cultivating self-acceptance. Surround yourself with people who uplift and support you in your journey toward self-acceptance.

In conclusion, accepting and embracing oneself is a lifelong journey. With these practical strategies, you can learn to embrace yourself wholly and cultivate self-love, leading to greater well-being and a more fulfilling life.

The Role of Self-Care

The term "self-care" has become increasingly popular in recent times due to its significance in maintaining or improving our physical, mental, and emotional health. Self-care includes various intentional actions and behaviors such as getting enough sleep and exercise, pursuing hobbies, and spending time with loved ones. Self-care is vital as neglecting our well-being can lead to negative consequences like decreased productivity, increased stress and anxiety, and physical and mental health problems. One of the significant benefits of self-care is its ability to manage stress. Chronic stress can cause severe health and well-being problems, and by engaging in self-care activities, we can relax and unwind, reduce stress levels, and improve our overall mood and outlook. Self-care can also improve our physical health by encouraging healthy behaviors such as eating a balanced diet, getting enough sleep, and regular exercise, which have a positive impact on our mental and emotional well-being. Additionally, taking care of ourselves can enhance our relationships with others as we become more compassionate, patient, and present, which can improve our connections with loved ones.

To prioritize our well-being and incorporate self-care into our daily routine, we can start by making self-care a priority and setting aside time each day for self-care activities. We should identify what self-care means to us, set realistic goals, practice self-compassion, and hold ourselves accountable. By making self-care a part of our lives, we can take care of ourselves and improve our overall health and well-being

Developing a Growth Mindset

A growth mindset is a way of thinking that involves believing in the idea that our abilities can be developed and improved over time. This is different from a fixed mindset, where we believe that our abilities are set and cannot be changed. Those with a growth mindset are more likely to be successful, resilient, and motivated. They view challenges as opportunities, failures as stepping stones, and approach life with curiosity and openness.

Having a growth mindset is important for several reasons. First, it enables us to embrace change and view challenges as chances for growth. With a growth mindset, we're not afraid to take risks or try new things because we recognize that failure is a natural part of the learning process. Secondly, a growth mindset helps us to bounce back from setbacks and failures. Instead of giving up or getting discouraged, we use those experiences as opportunities to learn and improve. Lastly, having a growth mindset allows us to achieve our goals and reach our full potential. When we believe that our abilities can be developed and improved over time, we are more likely to put in the effort and take the necessary steps to achieve our goals.

Developing a growth mindset takes time and effort, but anyone can do it. To get started, there are several tips that you can follow. First, embrace failure and view it as an opportunity to learn and improve. Second, focus on the process of learning and growing, rather than just the outcome. Third, adopt a "yet" mindset by acknowledging that you may not have the skills or knowledge right now, but you can learn and improve over time. Fourth, cultivate your own sense of curiosity by exploring new topics, trying new things, and asking questions. Finally, surround yourself with positive people who support your growth and development, such as mentors, coaches, and friends who encourage you to take risks, learn from your failures, and strive for your goals.

Overall, developing a growth mindset is about believing in your own ability to learn and grow, embracing change, and learning from failure. By adopting a growth mindset, you'll be better equipped to face challenges, bounce back from setbacks, and achieve your goals. Start small, focus on the process, and surround yourself with positive people who believe in your potential. With time and effort, you'll develop a growth mindset that will serve you well in all aspects of your life

Roles of compassion

Compassion is a powerful force that has the ability to transform our lives and the world around us. It is the ability to empathize with others and feel a deep concern for their well-being. Compassion is not just an emotion, but also an action. When we feel compassion for others, we're motivated to do something to help ease their suffering or improve their situation. In this interactive article, we will explore the role of compassion in our lives, why it's important, and how we can cultivate it within ourselves.

What is Compassion?

Compassion is often described as a feeling of empathy or sympathy for others who are suffering or experiencing difficulties. It is about being able to see things from another person's perspective and respond with kindness, care, and understanding. Compassion is not just about feeling sorry for someone or feeling their pain, it is about taking action to alleviate their suffering.

Compassion is a fundamental aspect of human connection and is essential for building positive relationships and fostering a sense of community. When we show compassion to others, we create a sense of connection and trust that can deepen over time. Compassion also helps us to navigate conflicts and resolve disagreements in a constructive and respectful manner.

Why is Compassion Important?

Compassion is important for a number of reasons. First, it's a key ingredient in building positive relationships. When we show compassion to others, we create a sense of connection and trust that can deepen over time. Compassion also helps us to navigate conflicts and resolve disagreements in a constructive and respectful manner.

Second, compassion is essential for promoting well-being and reducing stress. When we feel compassion for others, it can reduce our own feelings of anxiety and stress. Additionally, research has shown that people who show compassion tend to be more resilient and better able to cope with difficult situations.

Finally, compassion is important for creating a more just and equitable society. When we feel compassion for those who are marginalized or disadvantaged, we're more likely to take action to support them and advocate for their rights. Compassion is essential for building a more inclusive and compassionate world.

How to Cultivate Compassion

Cultivating compassion takes time and effort, but it's something that anyone can do. Here are some tips to help you get started:

Practice Mindfulness

1. Mindfulness is the practice of being present and fully engaged in the present moment. When we're mindful, we're more likely to notice the suffering of others and respond with compassion. Try incorporating mindfulness practices into your daily routine, such as meditation or deep breathing exercises.

Develop Empathy

2. Empathy is the ability to understand and share the feelings of others. Developing empathy can help us better to understand the experiences and perspectives of those around us, and respond with compassion. Try putting yourself in someone else's shoes and imagining how they might be feeling in a given situation.

Practice Active Listening

3. Active listening is a skill that involves fully focusing on the person who is speaking and paying attention to their words, body language, and tone of voice. When we practice active listening, we're more likely to understand the needs and concerns of others and respond with compassion.

Engage in Acts of Kindness

4.   Engaging in acts of kindness, no matter how small, can help to cultivate compassion. Try performing a random act of kindness for someone each day, such as holding the door open for someone, complimenting a coworker, or buying a cup of coffee for a stranger.

Volunteer and Give Back

5.   Volunteering and giving back to your community can be a powerful way to cultivate compassion. Look for opportunities to volunteer your time or donate to a charity that supports causes you care about.

By practicing mindfulness, developing empathy, engaging in acts of kindness, and giving back to your community,

Embracing your authentic self

Embracing your authentic self is about accepting and being true to who you are, rather than trying to fit into someone else's expectations or societal norms. It's about being comfortable in your own skin, embracing your strengths and weaknesses, and living your life with integrity and purpose. In this article, we'll explore why embracing your authentic self is important, the benefits it can bring, and how you can start to embrace your authentic self.

Why Embracing Your Authentic Self is Important

Embracing your authentic self is important for several reasons. Firstly, it can help you to feel more fulfilled and content in your life. When you're living in alignment with your values, beliefs, and passions, you're more likely to feel a sense of purpose and meaning in your life. This can help you to build greater self-confidence and resilience, and feel more comfortable expressing your true self. Secondly, embracing your authentic self can help you to build more fulfilling relationships. When you're being true to who you are, you're more likely to attract people into your life who appreciate and respect you for who you are. This can lead to more authentic, supportive, and fulfilling relationships.

Finally, embracing your authentic self can help you to make a positive impact in the world. When you're living in alignment with your values and passions, you're more likely to pursue opportunities that align with those values, and make a difference in the world. This can help you to live a more purposeful and fulfilling life, and create positive change in the world around you.

The Benefits of Embracing Your Authentic Self

Embracing your authentic self can bring many benefits to your life. Here are just a few:

1. Greater self-awareness: Embracing your authentic self requires you to be honest and introspective about who you are. This can help you to develop greater self-awareness and understanding, which can lead to personal growth and development.

2. Improved relationships: When you're being true to who you are, you're more likely to attract people into your life who appreciate and respect you for who you are. This can lead to more authentic, supportive, and fulfilling relationships.

3. Increased confidence: Embracing your authentic self can help you to build greater self-confidence and resilience. When you're comfortable in your own skin and living in alignment with your values, you're more likely to feel confident in yourself and your abilities.

4. Greater sense of purpose: Embracing your authentic self can help you to identify your values, passions, and purpose in life. This can help you to pursue opportunities that align with those values and make a positive impact in the world.

How to Embrace Your Authentic Self

Embracing your authentic self takes time and effort, but it's something that anyone can do. Here are some tips to help you get started:

1. Get to know yourself: Take time to reflect on your values, beliefs, and passions. What do you care about? What brings you joy and fulfillment? When you have a clear understanding of your authentic self, it's easier to live in alignment with those values.

2. Let go of expectations: Often, we feel pressure to live up to other people's expectations or societal norms. It's important to let go of these expectations and focus on being true to yourself. Remember that you don't need to please everyone, and it's okay to be different.

3. Practice self-compassion: Embracing your authentic self can be a challenging journey, and it's important to be kind to yourself along the way. Practice self-compassion and remind yourself that it's okay to make mistakes or have setbacks.

4. Set boundaries: When you're living in alignment with your authentic self, it's important to set boundaries and prioritize your

Boundaries

Boundaries are an integral aspect of our lives, serving as markers for what we are willing to tolerate from others. They can manifest in physical, emotional, or mental forms, and they are vital for preserving our well-being and safeguarding our interests.

Boundaries enable us to communicate our desires, limitations and needs to others, and they empower us to make informed and healthy decisions concerning our lives.

One of the primary reasons for setting boundaries is to protect our physical and emotional safety. Boundaries assist us in defining what we are prepared to accept regarding physical touch, verbal abuse, or emotional manipulation. By establishing clear boundaries, we decrease the risk of physical harm and emotional distress and ensure that our relationships remain healthy and positive.

Another significant rationale for creating boundaries is to maintain our individuality and independence. Boundaries help us to assert our independence and make autonomous decisions without undue influence or pressure from others. They also aid us in establishing mutually respectful and trustworthy relationships rather than ones based on control or manipulation.

Boundaries play a vital role in fostering healthy relationships with others. They enable us to communicate our requirements and expectations in a clear and effective manner, facilitating mutual comprehension and trust. By setting boundaries, we establish a sense of safety and security in our relationships, leading to greater intimacy and connection over time.

Furthermore, boundaries assist us in managing our time and energy more efficiently. By imposing limitations on our commitments and availability, we ensure that we have sufficient time and energy to care for ourselves, our relationships, and other responsibilities.

This helps us avoid burnout, stress, and overwhelm, allowing us to maintain a healthy work-life balance.

Boundaries also contribute to our mental health and well-being. By restricting our exposure to negative or toxic individuals or situations, we reduce our risk of depression, anxiety, or other mental health problems. Boundaries also help us cultivate healthy and positive relationships, which promote emotional and psychological growth and resilience.

Establishing boundaries can be challenging, especially if we are not accustomed to advocating for ourselves or setting limits with others. However, it is a critical skill to develop, and there are numerous strategies and techniques to do so effectively.

One of the most important strategies for setting boundaries is to be explicit and direct about our expectations and requirements. This may entail expressing our boundaries calmly and assertively, using "I" statements to articulate our own needs and feelings, and avoiding blame or criticism of others.

Another crucial strategy is to be consistent in our boundary-setting behavior. This may entail setting precise limits and consequences for unacceptable behavior and following through on these limits and consequences consistently over time. This helps us establish a sense of predictability and safety in our relationships, promoting trust and respect.

It is also crucial to be flexible in our approach to setting boundaries and willing to negotiate and compromise with others when necessary. This may involve being open to feedback and suggestions from others and being willing to adapt our boundaries as our needs and circumstances change over time.

In conclusion, boundaries are a fundamental component of our lives, and they play a crucial role in maintaining our physical, emotional, and mental well-being. By establishing clear and consistent boundaries with others, we assert our individuality, promote healthy relationships, and safeguard our safety and autonomy. Developing effective boundary-setting skills may take time and practice, but it is a crucial investment in our personal growth and happiness.

Harnessing Your Inner Strength

When it comes to harnessing your inner strength, there are a number of approaches you can take. Here are five key strategies that can help you tap into your inner resources and build the resilience and confidence you need to achieve your goals.

1. Reflection Questions

One of the first steps in harnessing your inner strength is to understand your natural talents, abilities, and challenges. By reflecting on your experiences, you can identify the things that have helped you succeed in the past, as well as the obstacles you've overcome.

To get started, ask yourself some reflection questions, such as:

- What are some of my natural talents or abilities?
- What are some challenges I have faced in the past and how did I overcome them?
- What motivates me to keep pushing forward even when things get tough?
- What are some values that I hold dear and how do they guide my actions?

Take some time to reflect on these questions and write down your answers. You can also discuss your responses with a trusted friend or mentor to gain additional insights.

2.   Positive Affirmations

Positive affirmations are another powerful tool for harnessing your inner strength. Affirmations are positive statements that help you build self-confidence and tap into your inner resources. By repeating these affirmations to yourself each day, you can train your mind to focus on positive outcomes and cultivate a sense of inner strength.

Some examples of positive affirmations include:

- "I am strong and capable of overcoming any challenge."
- "I trust in my abilities to achieve my goals."
- "I am resilient and can bounce back from setbacks."

Repeat these affirmations to yourself each day, either out loud or in your mind. You can also write them down and post them somewhere visible as a reminder.

3.   Visualization Exercises

Visualization exercises can help you tap into your inner strength by imagining yourself succeeding in a specific situation. By visualizing success, you can build confidence and reduce anxiety about upcoming challenges.

To do a visualization exercise, find a quiet place where you can relax and focus. Close your eyes and visualize the situation in detail, using all of your senses to make it feel as real as possible. Spend a few minutes in this visualization, imagining yourself succeeding and feeling empowered.

For example, if you have a big presentation coming up at work, try visualizing yourself giving the presentation with confidence and poise. Imagine the audience responding positively to your ideas and feeling inspired by your message.

4.   Goal Setting

Setting goals is another powerful way to harness your inner strength. By setting meaningful goals and breaking them down into smaller, achievable steps, you can build momentum and make progress towards your dreams.

To get started, choose a goal that is important to you, such as running a marathon, learning a new skill, or achieving a professional milestone. Break this goal down into smaller, achievable steps, such as running a mile each day or setting aside time to practice your new skill.

As you work towards your goal, celebrate your progress along the way. Each small achievement will help build your confidence and inner strength.

5.   Accountability Partners

Finally, finding an accountability partner can be a powerful way to harness your inner strength. By working with someone who shares your values and can provide encouragement and guidance, you can stay motivated and make progress towards your goals.

This could be a friend, family member, or mentor who you trust and respect. Set regular check-ins with your accountability partner to share your progress and receive feedback.

In conclusion, harnessing your inner strength requires a combination of self-reflection, positive affirmations, visualization exercises, goal setting, and accountability partnerships. By practicing these strategies regularly, you can build the resilience and confidence you need to achieve your dreams. Remember, building inner strength takes time and practice, but with dedication and perseverance, you can achieve great

The Power of Forgiveness

Forgiveness is a complex and multifaceted process that involves letting go of negative emotions such as anger, resentment, and bitterness toward someone who has hurt us. It is a decision to release the desire for revenge and choose to move forward with a greater sense of peace and freedom. Forgiveness can bring numerous benefits to our lives, including improved relationships, reduced stress and anxiety, enhanced emotional intelligence, increased self-esteem, and improved physical health.

One of the most significant benefits of forgiveness is improved relationships. When we forgive someone, we let go of negative emotions that may have been causing tension or conflict in the relationship. This can allow us to communicate more openly and honestly, leading to greater understanding and trust between us. However, forgiveness does not necessarily mean that we have to maintain a relationship with the offender. It is possible to forgive someone and choose to end the relationship if it is not healthy or beneficial for us.

Forgiveness can also reduce stress and anxiety. Carrying feelings of anger, resentment, and bitterness can be incredibly stressful and can lead to anxiety and other mental health issues. Forgiveness allows us to release these negative emotions, reducing our stress levels and improving our overall well-being. By letting go of negative emotions, we can focus on positive thoughts and feelings that can help us to feel more relaxed and content.

Another benefit of forgiveness is enhanced emotional intelligence. Forgiveness requires empathy and understanding toward the offender. When we practice forgiveness, we develop our emotional intelligence, which is the ability to understand and manage our own emotions as well as the emotions of others. Forgiveness involves recognizing and acknowledging the emotions of the offender and ourselves. This can help us to develop a greater sense of compassion and understanding towards others.

Forgiveness can also increase our self-esteem. Forgiving someone who has hurt us can be incredibly empowering. It allows us to take control of our emotions and our lives, rather than allowing the offender to continue to have power over us. This can lead to increased self-esteem and confidence. When we forgive someone, we are able to focus on our own needs and well-being, which can lead to a greater sense of self-worth.

Finally, forgiveness can improve our physical health. Research has shown that practicing forgiveness can lead to improved physical health. Forgiveness can reduce stress, which in turn can improve our immune system function, lower our blood pressure, and reduce our risk of heart disease. When we forgive, we are able to let go of negative emotions that can have a detrimental effect on our physical health.

Despite these numerous benefits, forgiveness can be difficult to practice. It requires us to let go of negative emotions and choose to move forward with a sense of compassion and understanding. Here are some tips for practicing forgiveness:

Firstly, it is important to acknowledge your emotions. Forgiveness doesn't mean denying or suppressing your emotions. It's important to acknowledge and process the pain and hurt caused by the offense. This can involve talking to a trusted friend or therapist, writing in a journal, or engaging in other forms of self-care. By acknowledging our emotions, we can begin to understand why we are feeling the way we are and work towards finding a way to let go of those emotions.

Secondly, gaining empathy and understanding toward the offender can be a powerful tool in forgiving. Try to put yourself in their shoes and understand their perspective. This doesn't mean excusing their behavior, but rather acknowledging that they may have been acting out of their own pain or hurt. By understanding why the offender acted the way they did, we can begin to find compassion and understanding towards them.

Thirdly, forgiveness is a conscious choice. It may not happen overnight, but it's important to make the decision to release negative emotions toward the offender and to choose to move forward with a greater sense of peace and freedom.

Mindfulness

Mindfulness and self-awareness are two powerful practices that can help us live more fulfilling lives. Both practices involve paying attention to our thoughts, emotions, and physical sensations with an attitude of curiosity and openness. When we combine mindfulness and self-awareness, we can gain a greater sense of clarity and focus in our lives, which can lead to improved decision-making, increased emotional regulation, enhanced communication skills, greater resilience, and more.

One of the key benefits of mindfulness and self-awareness is improved decision-making. When we practice mindfulness and self-awareness, we become more attuned to our thoughts and emotions. This can help us make more informed and thoughtful decisions, based on our own values and priorities. We become more aware of the choices we make and the impact they have on ourselves and others. We are able to take a step back and assess our situation before reacting impulsively, and this can lead to better outcomes.

Another benefit of mindfulness and self-awareness is increased emotional regulation. By recognizing and acknowledging our emotions, we can choose how to respond to them in a way that aligns with our values and goals. We become more aware of our emotional triggers and can choose to respond to them in a way that is constructive rather than destructive. We become more in control of our emotions and this helps us to manage stress more effectively.

Practicing mindfulness and self-awareness can also help us become better communicators. By being fully present and attentive to others, we can listen more effectively and respond in a way that is empathetic and understanding. We become more aware of our own communication style and how it affects others. This can lead to greater understanding and fewer misunderstandings in our relationships.

Another benefit of mindfulness and self-awareness is greater resilience. By being aware of our thoughts and emotions, we can choose to respond in a way that is positive and constructive, rather than letting negative emotions overwhelm us. We become more resilient in the face of challenges and setbacks, and this helps us to bounce back more quickly from adversity.

So how can we practice mindfulness and self-awareness in our daily lives? There are many ways to cultivate these skills, and different practices work for different people. Some simple practices include mindful breathing, meditation, journaling, mindful movement, increased self-compassion, better sleep, greater gratitude, and improved relationships.

One of the simplest ways to practice mindfulness is through mindful breathing. This involves taking a few moments each day to focus on your breath, noticing the sensation of air moving in and out of your body. This can be done anywhere, anytime, and is a great way to bring yourself back to the present moment and reduce stress.

Regular meditation practice can help us develop greater mindfulness and self-awareness. Find a quiet place to sit and focus on your breath, allowing thoughts and emotions to come and go without judgment. This can be challenging at first, but with practice, it becomes easier and can lead to greater clarity and focus.

Writing down our thoughts and emotions can help us gain greater self-awareness. Take a few moments each day to reflect on your experiences, noting any patterns or themes that emerge. This can help us to recognize our triggers and patterns of behavior, and make positive changes in our lives.

Mindful movement, such as yoga, tai chi, and walking, can help us cultivate mindfulness and self-awareness. Focus on the sensations in your body as you move, and allow your mind to be fully present at the moment. This can be a great way to reduce stress, increase flexibility, and improve overall physical health.

Cultivating self-compassion is another important practice for developing mindfulness and self-awareness. This involves treating ourselves with kindness and understanding, rather than judgment and criticism. By recognizing our own struggles and challenges, we can respond to ourselves with empathy.

Cultivating Meaningful Connections

Mindfulness and self-awareness can play a crucial role in improving various aspects of our lives, including self-compassion, sleep quality, gratitude, and relationships. By cultivating these skills, we can lead happier and more fulfilling lives.

Self-compassion involves treating ourselves with kindness and understanding, rather than judgment and criticism. By recognizing our own struggles and challenges, we can respond to ourselves with empathy and compassion, rather than self-blame and shame. Mindfulness and self-awareness can help us cultivate self-compassion by enabling us to focus on our inner experiences and emotions without judgment. We can use mindfulness techniques such as deep breathing or meditation to calm our minds and bodies and promote a more compassionate self-dialogue.

Sleep quality is another important aspect of our overall well-being that can be improved through mindfulness and self-awareness. By practicing mindfulness techniques before bed, we can reduce stress and promote relaxation, leading to a more restful night's sleep. This can include activities such as deep breathing, visualization, or meditation, which help us calm our minds and prepare for a peaceful sleep.

Gratitude is another positive trait that can be enhanced through mindfulness and self-awareness. By focusing on the positive aspects of our lives and expressing gratitude for them, we can cultivate a more positive outlook and greater happiness. We can practice gratitude by reflecting on the things we are thankful for in our lives and expressing our appreciation for them.

Finally, mindfulness and self-awareness can help us build better relationships with others by improving our communication skills, increasing our empathy and understanding, and reducing conflict and misunderstandings. When we are present and engaged in our interactions with others, we are better able to listen and understand their perspectives. We can also practice empathy by putting ourselves in others' shoes and validating their feelings and experiences.

Cultivating meaningful connections with others is essential for our overall well-being. Research has shown that having strong connections with others can improve our mental, emotional, and physical health. Meaningful connections can also increase our resilience in the face of challenges and setbacks and contribute to our overall happiness and life satisfaction.

To cultivate meaningful connections with others, we can practice several practical strategies. Being present and fully engaged in our interactions with others is essential for building deeper and more meaningful relationships. We can also practice empathy by actively listening and validating others' experiences. Looking for common ground and shared interests can also help us connect with others on a deeper level.

Volunteering or joining a group can be a great way to meet new people and build connections. Whether we volunteer at a local charity or join a community group, we'll have the opportunity to connect with others who share our interests and values. Expressing gratitude and forgiveness can also help us build stronger connections with others, as we learn to appreciate and accept others for who they are.

Finally, cultivating meaningful connections with others requires us to be authentic and true to ourselves. When we are open and honest about our thoughts, feelings, and experiences, we create opportunities for deeper, more meaningful connections with others. By practicing mindfulness and self-awareness regularly, we can develop these skills and create greater peace and happiness in our lives

www.ingramcontent.com/pod-product-compliance
Lightning Source LLC
Chambersburg PA
CBHW061558250726
48657CB00021B/2309